THE COTTAGE HOTEL SONGBOOK

Azalea Art Press
Sonoma | California

© Karen Mireau, 2023.

ISBN: 978-1-943471-72-0

Cover Art:
Kim Ormiston

for
Hilary & David Stott
& all who love the music
at the *Cottage Hotel of Mendon*

CONTENTS

Preface i

(You'll Never Feel Alone)
at the Cottage Hotel 1
by Steve Anderson

Powder Mill 6
by Steve Anderson

This Song 11
by Keith Baker

One Horse Town 15
by Johnny Bauer

On Cobblestone Fields 19
by Brian Venton

Good Old Days 23
by Jeff Williams

About the Musicians 27

Music Videos 38

Acknowledgments 39

Contact / To Order 40

Preface

The original tunes that appear in this book
were written about the *Cottage Hotel*,
a 200-year-old stagecoach inn and tavern
in Mendon hamlet in Upstate New York.

You might call each a tribute
to the collective heart of our younger days,
evoking a specific place and time that will
live on long after we are gone.

The musicians who wrote them
and the bands that performed them
deserve our eternal respect and applause.
They invited us all to get up and dance,
to feel life fully, to love and be loved.

Their beautiful, passionate, creative energy
was and is a pure magnetic force
that keeps us coming back for more.

Here, now are their tributes to
the *Cottage Hotel*.

Steve Anderson

(You'll Never Feel Alone) at the Cottage Hotel[1]
by Steve Anderson

Verse 1:

```
C
```
I'm sittin' here at this bar,
```
        F            C
```
drinking Tanqueray and tonics.
```
F           C
```
Glass filled full of stars, heart filled full of stones.
```
    C       F       C
```
I've always been a dreamer, out there alone.
```
    F         C           G
```
So I set down the glass, pick up my phone.

```
F       C  F      C
```
"Hey, it's me. I'm at the Cottage.
```
F       C       G
```
Yeah that's right. I know, big surprise.
```
C
```
So many roads we have travelled,
```
    F           C
```
the children have all grown
```
    F           C
```
But sittin' here at this bar,
```
    G       C
```
it still feels like home."

---

[1] *(You'll Never Feel Alone) at the Cottage Hotel* © Steve Anderson, 2019.

(Chorus)

C
So raise your glass.
    F   C
A toast to our lost loved ones.
              F   C
May they always walk among us.
G
Be our shining light.
        C   F   C
Every person here tonight has a story to tell.
F   C   G   C
You'll never be alone at the Cottage Hotel.

Verse 2:

C
I see John behind the bar,
    F   C
he's laughin' with Craiger.
F   C   G
Laurie's at the door, in comes Space Invaders.
C
Jimmy's playing Foosball,
F   C
Jeff's up on the stage.
F   C   G
And now everybody's dancin',
   G   C
but hey, it's gettin' late.
C   F   G
So one more drink, then I'll let go.

```
F                    C
```
I just wanted to let you know.
```
        F            C
```
That I will always love you.
```
F              C
```
Please remember that.
```
F                    C
```
May the winds of good fortune
```
     G          C
```
be always at your back.

(Chorus)

Verse 3:

```
C
```
I'm still sittin' at this bar,
```
F              C
```
when you walk in door.
```
F                    G
```
That smile upon your face, might be my saving grace.
```
C                    F        C
```
Come now sit beside me, rest your weary bones.
```
C                    F
```
We'll talk of trains and summer rain
```
C              G
```
and places yet to roam.
```
F        C      F    C
```
It's closing time, it's time I go.

```
F         C              G
```
But I'll be back next time around.
```
F            C    F         C
```
Until we meet again, I wish you well.
```
F            C    G            C
```
The prettiest girls are at the Cottage Hotel.

(Chorus)

```
C
```
So raise your glass.
```
    F              C
```
A toast to our lost loved ones.
```
           F                  C
```
May they always walk among us.
```
G
```
Be our shining light.
```
      C                  F       C
```
Every person here tonight has a story to tell.
```
F           C    G       C
```
You'll never be alone at the Cottage Hotel.

```
F           C       G     C
```
You'll never be alone at the Cottage Hotel.
```
F           C       G     C
```
You'll never be alone at the Cottage Hotel.
```
F           C       G     C
```
You'll never be alone at the Cottage Hotel.

Steve Anderson

Powder Mill[2]

by Steve Anderson

Verse 1:

```
 C#m         A              E
A church bell rings down in the village.
 C#m    A         E
A smile, oft-remembered well.
 C#m     A           E
Flowers bloom along the towpath,
 C#m          B          A   E
As we drift on down along the old canal.
 B                  E
I see you standin' at Four Corners.
   B                E
A certain sadness in your eyes.
 B             E       A
Colonial Days parade, seems like yesterday.
                         B
Never had the chance to say goodbye.
```

(Chorus)

```
 E       B      E
Walk with us into the summer.
 E          B     E
Meet us down at Powder Mill.
```

---

[2] *Powder Mill* © Steve Anderson, 2019.

```
E                        A
We'll drink some beers, count the years.
E          B             A
We love you now, and always will.
```

Verse 2:

```
C#m           A            E
There's no more milk down at the Milk Store.
C#m           A         E
In the Basin, just passin' through?
C#m           A              E
Or maybe we all just dreamt the same dream –
C#m           B      A   E
Somewhere, beyond the moon?
```

(Chorus)

Verse 3:

```
C#m           A            E
Creek's run dry down by the Mill Wheel.
C#m           A              E
Skippin' school, but still passed the test.
C#m           A            E
Ever sweeter for the leaving, my friend.
C#m           A            E
Walk with your ghosts in Shady Rest.
```

(Chorus)

Verse 4:

```
C#m              A            E
```
Fish are jumpin' down at the hatchery.
```
C#m              A                  E
```
The leaves have turned from green to gold.
```
C#m         A            E
```
Maybe we see the way things used to be.
```
C#m                 A           E
```
Or maybe we're all just getting old.

(Chorus)

Verse 5:

```
C#m            A           E
```
Thought I saw you drinkin' whiskey.
```
C#m           A        E
```
At the ol' hotel, after the fair.
```
C#m           A          E
```
But then the band begins to play,
```
C#m         A       E
```
and it all just fades away . . .
```
C#m            A            E
```
Let sweet soulful songs fill the air.

(a cappella Chorus)

*John Paulsen, Keith Baker
& John Garvey*

This Song[3]

by Keith Baker

Verse 1:

Bm
You heard the group was really good.
      A
You'd like to see them, if you could
        G   F#
so you brought along a dozen friends or more.
Bm
When you arrived, the man said, "Wait!"
      A
that you'd arrived a little late.
      G   E   A
"There's only standing room, out on the floor."

(Chorus)

G   A
Then, this song goes out to you,
    D   G
in the back room, by the back door,
    D   A
by the Foosball table, by the juke box, by the bar.
G   A   D   Bm
Yeah! This song goes out to those who don't know it,
D   G   A   Bm
'cause they can't hear me sing it, where they are.

---

[3] *This Song* © Keith W. Baker, 1978, 2023.

Verse 2:

Bm
You love someone who's in the band.
     A
He's tall good looking and well-tanned.
    G   *F#*
He smiles at you and sings your favorite song.
Bm
You hear him singing that song now.
     A
You'd like to see him, if somehow
   G   *E*   *A*
the crowd in front of you would move along.

(Chorus)
&
(Refrain)

G   *A*   *D*
Well, it's nice to go out for some music.
      G   *D*
and it's nice to sit down with a beer.
     G   *A*   *D*   *Bm*
It's nice to share a song and, maybe, sing along.
     G   *A*   *Bm*
It's too bad when you can't even hear.

Verse 3:

     Bm
They play the music, that you love,
    A
still, you don't like to push and shove,
    G   F#
well, now they're at a concert hall, that's near.
     Bm
The tickets cost you 80 bucks.
A
She buys a gown, you rent a tux,
    G   E   A   A7
but in the back row, you can hardly hear.

(Chorus)

G   A
Then, this song goes out to you,
     D   G
in the back room, by the back door,
    D   A
by the Foosball table, by the juke box, by the bar.
G   A   D   Bm
Yeah! This song goes out to those who don't know it,
D   G   A   Bm
'cause they can't hear me sing it, where they are.

Johnny Bauer

One Horse Town[4]

by Johnny Bauer

Verse 1:

```
D              A
Some people came for me
Bm         A         G
While others just came to eat
G    D                    Em       A
I overheard her say," I hope he's not too loud".
D         A
As the night goes on
Bm        A         G
And I'm strumming along
G        D          Em         A
Looks like it's gonna be a pretty good crowd
A        G
Then the drinks start to flow
             D
And the tips start to grow
Em                              A
All I can think is I hope she likes me
```

(Chorus)

```
D                       A
Another beer another shot
A     Em         G
Gonna give it all I've got
```

_____

[4] *One Horse Town* © Johnny Bauer, 2012.

```
   D            A       G
To play you your favorite songs
G     D        A
At the end of the night
                   Em    G
When everyone is feeling alright
          D           A      E
And the jukebox plays on and on
G                    A
Until next week rolls around
G                       A
I'll be back, back in this one horse town
```

Verse 2:

```
D                      A
There's a girl at the bar
           Bm      A
Watching me play guitar
       G     D    Em     A
I can tell that she'd love to dance
           D         A
There's a guy named Jim
         Bm      A
With a wide eyed grin
G           D      Em     A
Thinking that he might stand a chance
            G
Then the beer starts to flow
         D
And the tips start to grow
Em                        A
All I can think is I hope they like me
```

(Chorus)

Verse 3:

D   A
When the night draws to an end
         Bm   A
I pick up my gear again
G   D   EM   A
Hear the bartender yell last call for alcohol
         G
Have a toast with my friends
              D
May these nights never end
EM   A
With this I make my solemn vow

(Chorus)

D   A
Another beer another shot
A   Em   G
Gonna give it all I've got
       D   A   G
To play you your favorite songs
G   D   A
At the end of the night
                  Em   G
When everyone is feeling alright
            D   A   E
And the jukebox plays on and on
G   A
Until next week rolls around
G   A
I'll be back, back in this one horse town

Autumn Skies
*Mark Smith, Brian Venton, Scott Brown (kneeling),
and Randy Stuckless (standing)*

On Cobblestone Fields[5]

by Brian Venton

(a capella)

It was a time, was a time
It was a time, oh what a time it was

(Intro:)

Asus2   E   Asus2   B9sus2   E

Verse 1:

A   Amaj7   Am
Late '70-something, as fortunes would tell
A   Amaj7   Dsus4
We all had a voice, we all found our song
A   Amaj7   Am7
Strummers and singers, played on, played well
A   B9sus2   E
We ushered in angels, and flirted with hell

A   Amaj7   Am
Of drovers and drummers, a silent dove sings
A   Amaj7   Dsus4
The river rolled on, the flow was so sweet
A   Amaj7   Am7
To celebrate life, on open wings
A   B9sus2   E
Aching with love, for better things

(Chorus:)

---

[5] *On Cobblestone Fields* © Brian Venton, 2023.

```
          F#m7           Cmaj7                    E
```
In the Cottage, on the corner, of Cobblestone Fields
```
        Asus2       Cmaj7
```
It was a time, was a time
```
        Asus2                   E
```
It was a time, oh what a time it was

Verse 2:

```
A              Amaj7         Am
```
With love in the music, spirits run wild
```
A              Amaj7            Dsus4
```
The timing was perfect, a symphony score
```
A              Amaj7           Am7
```
Locals and newbies, a laugh and a smile
```
A          B9sus2         E
```
All in one head, at least for that while

```
A              Amaj7         Am
```
After a show, at Burdock's old place
```
A              Amaj7       Dsus4
```
We danced under the stars, with freedom and grace
```
A              Amaj7            Am7
```
Before the sun peeked, with warmest goodbyes
```
A          B9sus2         E
```
We bid final farewell, to those warm smiling eyes

(Chorus:)

```
          F#m7           Cmaj7                    E
```
In the Cottage, on the corner, of Cobblestone Fields
```
        Asus2       Cmaj7
```
It was a time, was a time
```
        Asus2                   E
```
It was a time, oh what a time it was

(Courtesy: Brian Lyons.)

Earl Weems Revue
*Mike Archer, Kerry Keating, Dave Helander,
John Chaffer, Earl Weems (Jeff Williams), Hap Harrison
(missing are Ed Kosenski & Pete Freeman)*

Good Old Days[6]

by Jeff Williams

(Intro:)

F   F#dim7   C/G   Am   B flat   G   C

Verse 1:

C
I think a lot about the good old days
      G
when I was back in Honeoye Falls
      C
About sticky summer days and cold winter nights,
    C
but that's not what I like to recall.
C
I can't forget about the days with ZBB
        F   F#dim7
and good rockin' with ol' Billy Jones
        G
I used to spend a lot of nights down at Bates pond
      G   C
with the people I could call my own

(Chorus:)

---

[6] *Good Old Days* © Jeffrey D. Williams, 2023.

C
Those old days were good old days,
    B flat   G   C
but these are pretty good days, too.
C
I may be a little bit older, a wee bit wiser,
   D7   G
but I can't choose between the two.
     F   F#dim7   C/G   Am
I don't know which I like better, but that's okay, too,
    F   F#dim7   C/G   Am
'cause those old days were good old days
   B flat   G   C
but these are pretty good days, too.

Verse 2:

C
Well, you could hear a radio show,
                 G
live stereo with Rockin' Red or Roomful of Blues
G
Playin' in a bar on a fat guitar
                   C
that's liable to be hot enough to light any fuse.
C
If I went back today it wouldn't be the same,
   F   F#dim7
but I got lots of friends who remember
         G
That if you raise enough hell at the *Cottage Hotel*
    G   C
you can keep the place warm in December.

```
       F                    G
Pretty good times! Pretty good times!
```

(Bridge:)

```
        Am              Am/G#    Am/G
Well, thinkin' 'bout the days that used to be
     F
is fun but you gotta move on
        Am       Am/G#         Am/G  Am/F#
Gotta live for today and leave the past   alone
         F
you'll be wishin' your life away
         Am
Hey-yay, yeah!
```

(Guitar solo)

(Repeat chorus(es)

About the Musicians

Dave Knight, Jeff Decker, Chris Cady, Joe West, Steve Anderson

Steve Anderson
& Slipton Fell

*Steve Anderson - guitars, vocals | Chris Cady - guitars, vocals
Kit Cady - keyboards | Brian Cusimano - guitar
Mark DeAngelis - drums | Jeff Decker - guitar, vocals
Dave Knight - bass | Jessie Knight - vocals |
Korie Pettee - keyboards, vocals
Don Torpy - bass | Joe West - drums, percussion, vocals*

Slipton Fell was formed by Pittsford-Mendon High School students Chris Cady, Steve Anderson, Mark DeAngelis, Dave Knight, and Jeff Decker, who added many original tunes to their repertoire. Their original songs plus excellent covers of *Grateful Dead*, *Tom Petty*, and *Little Feat* songs kept us all rocking. When Mark and Dave left the band, Joe West and Don Torpy became members. Sadly, Jeff Decker died in 2004 and Mark DeAngelis in 2021. Dave's daughter, Jessie Knight, joined them in 2012, as did Chris' niece, Kit Cady. Their newest member since 2022 is Korie Pettee. *Slipton Fell* officially played as a band from August 13, 1978 to New Year's Eve in 1981—only 3 1/2 years—but since 1982 they have played reunions and continue to do so today.

Visit Slipton Fell's FaceBook page at:
https://www.facebook.com/SliptonFellBand

Check out Steve Anderson's website at:
www.steveandersonfilm.com

**For bookings, please contact:
Chris Cady at 404-610-3007 or ccady111@gmail.com**

John Paulsen & Keith Baker

Keith Baker
Paulsen, Baker & Garvey
Paulsen, Baker, Garvey & Keltz
The Paulsen & Baker Band

John Paulsen – vocals, acoustic guitar & electric guitar, banjo, harmonica, fiddle

Keith Baker – vocals, rhythm guitar, mandolin & (occasional) percussion

John Garvey – vocals, electric bass, & conductor

Al Keltz – Vocals, lead guitar (electric & acoustic) & pedal steel guitar (mid - ten years with the band)

Jeff Schrom – percussion (mid – ten years with the band)

Tim Chaapel – vocals, stand-up bass (occasional guitar and/or mandolin) (last eight years with the band)

Warren Paul – vocals, guitar, bass, (occasional band member, last eight years)

Since 1974, the country-folk-rock "goodtime music" of Paulsen, Baker & Garvey has been entertaining audiences at the *Cottage Hotel*.

Although John Garvey left the group seven years ago, John Paulsen and Keith Baker continue to perform along with special guests such as Tim Chaapel and Warren Paul.

Paulsen and Baker continue to delight and amuse us with their trademark humor, something that has always set them apart from other musicians.

View their website at:
http://pbgband.com

For bookings, please contact:
jpaulsen@rochester.rr.com or call 585-657-6950

Johnny Bauer & Nicki Paris

Johnny Bauer
& the Johnny Bauer Band

Johnny Bauer – *guitar, vocals* | ***Nicki Paris*** – *bass, vocals*
Ryan Bauer – *drums, guitar, vocals*

Johnny Bauer has been a musician and entertainer since he was three years old. His father, Charlie; his mother, Dee; his brothers Chuck and Dan; and his sister DeAnna, all performed together as the band *Bauer Power*.

Johnny began experimenting with guitar in high school, later playing with his father and brothers in the band *Mentor* in the 1980s. A serious music career ensued in his twenties. After the birth of his two sons, Johnny embarked on an ambitious new chapter as a solo acoustic performer in Rochester, New York, performing over 250 shows a year. From rock to blues to country, his repertoire includes over 200 original songs.

He now performs with his partner and bandmate Nicki Paris, whom he met and fell in love with at *The Cottage Hotel*! Nicki plays the bass and sings, while Johnny plays the guitar, writes the music, and sings. Johnny's son, Ryan, who has his own musical career, performs with them sometimes on either drums or guitar as well as vocals. His other son, Elijah, is special needs and enjoys the music of the Johnny Bauer Band.

Visit him on his website at:
https://www.johnnybauer.com

and on FaceBook at:
https://www.facebook.com/johnnybauermusic

For bookings, please contact:
johnnybauerjab@gmail.com

Brian Venton

Brian Venton
& Autumn Skies | Venton Clark Band

Autumn Skies
Mark Smith – drums, vocals | *Brian Venton* – bass, guitar, trumpet, vocals
Scott Brown – guitar, vocals | *Randy Stuckless* – guitar, bass, mandolin, vocals

Venton Clark Band
Brian Venton – vocals, guitar, bass | *Jeff Clark* – vocals, guitar
Steve Krauss – vocals, drums

In 1977, when he was 17, Brian Venton began performing at *The Cottage* as the lead of the group *Autumn Skies*.

That spring the band made a 45 record that attracted an agent, Pelican Productions, and for two years they played all over New York state. *The Cottage* was their first professional gig, and later on, they also played regularly at the *Mason Jar*, and numerous other venues across western New York.

From the early '80s, Brian created a succession of bands such as *NIK & The Nice Guys*, *The Boss Street Band*, and *Keys to the Caddy*. But his favorite gig was always the *Cottage Hotel*.

A chance meeting with Jeff Clark in 2018 led Brian to form the acoustic-rock *Venton Clark Band*, that now play at *The Cottage* once a month along with Steve Krauss (of Mendon) on drums and sometimes additional musicians.

**Contact Brian at:
ventonclarkband@gmail.com**

Jeff Williams
(Photo by: Chris Shaffer.)

Jeff Williams
Earl Weems Revue

***Jeff Williams** – guitar, vocals* | ***Kerry Keating** – keyboards*
***Hap Harrison** – pedal steel guitar* | ***Mike Archer** – guitar*
***Dave Helander** – bass* | ***John Chaffer** – drums*
***Ed Kosenski** – sax* | ***Pete Freeman** – pedal steel guitar (1977)*

Jeff Williams, founding member of *Earl Weems Revue,* first picked up a guitar at age twelve. Before long he formed a band with two other Honeoye Falls students — blues guitarist John Mooney and drummer Jesse Presto.

By age 20, Jeff was playing as the *Burned Out Blues Band* with drummer John Chaffer, guitarist Bill Jones, and Dave Helander on bass. They kept adding band members and from 1976-1978 performed as the *Earl Weems Revue* (named after his grandmother's pronunciation of their last name Williams as 'Weeyums'). The 'Earl' part was a direct nod to Earl Scruggs, who at the time had a band with two of his sons — the Earl Scruggs Revue.

The last edition of the *Revue* had seven players. It was definitely a Big Band sound with a very eclectic mix of Blues, R&B, Western Swing, and Country Rock. It was great dance music — lots of people showed up to do swing dancing. Some of their live gigs were broadcast on WCMF.

For the last 32 years, Jeff has been a music teacher. Since 2000, he has recorded as *Jeffrey D & the J-Dubs*. He performs with the *Coolrays* and with the *Jackstraws* (Jeff Willams, Loren Smith and Jeff Bristol), in the San Diego area, where he now lives.

Listen to his song
Good Old Days at:
https://soundcloud.com/jeffrey-d-1/goodolddays

Music Videos

Steve Anderson:

(You'll Never Feel Alone) at The Cottage Hotel
https://www.youtube.com/watch?v=pffVf0fqb94.

Powder Mill
https://www.youtube.com/watch?v=38p8KuD3HzY.

☙ ☙ ☙

Keith Baker:

This Song
sung by John Paulsen, Keith Baker, & Tim Chappell
https://www.youtube.com/watch?v=HTm0GXarkX8.

☙ ☙ ☙

Johnny Bauer:

One Horse Town
https://www.youtube.com/watch?v=EIQnD8cGGCU.

☙ ☙ ☙

Brian Venton:

https://www.facebook.com/ventonclarkband/videos/5500729750004401.

☙ ☙ ☙

Jeff Williams & the Jackstraws:

https://www.youtube.com/watch?v=IhLldtvl4YI.

Acknowledgments

My heartfelt thanks to the musicians
who so generously shared their songs,
photographs, and stories with us.

My gratitude especially to
Hilary and David Stott, owners
of the *Cottage Hotel of Mendon*,
who graciously brought us all together
in celebration of these original tunes.

These songs are the soundtrack
of the lives of those of us
who have had the good fortune
to hear and dance to the amazing bands
at the *Cottage Hotel*.

They and their music
will never be forgotten.

*To Contact the Publisher
please email:
Azalea.Art.Press@gmail.com*

*For Direct Book Orders
please visit:
www.Lulu.com*